I0821318

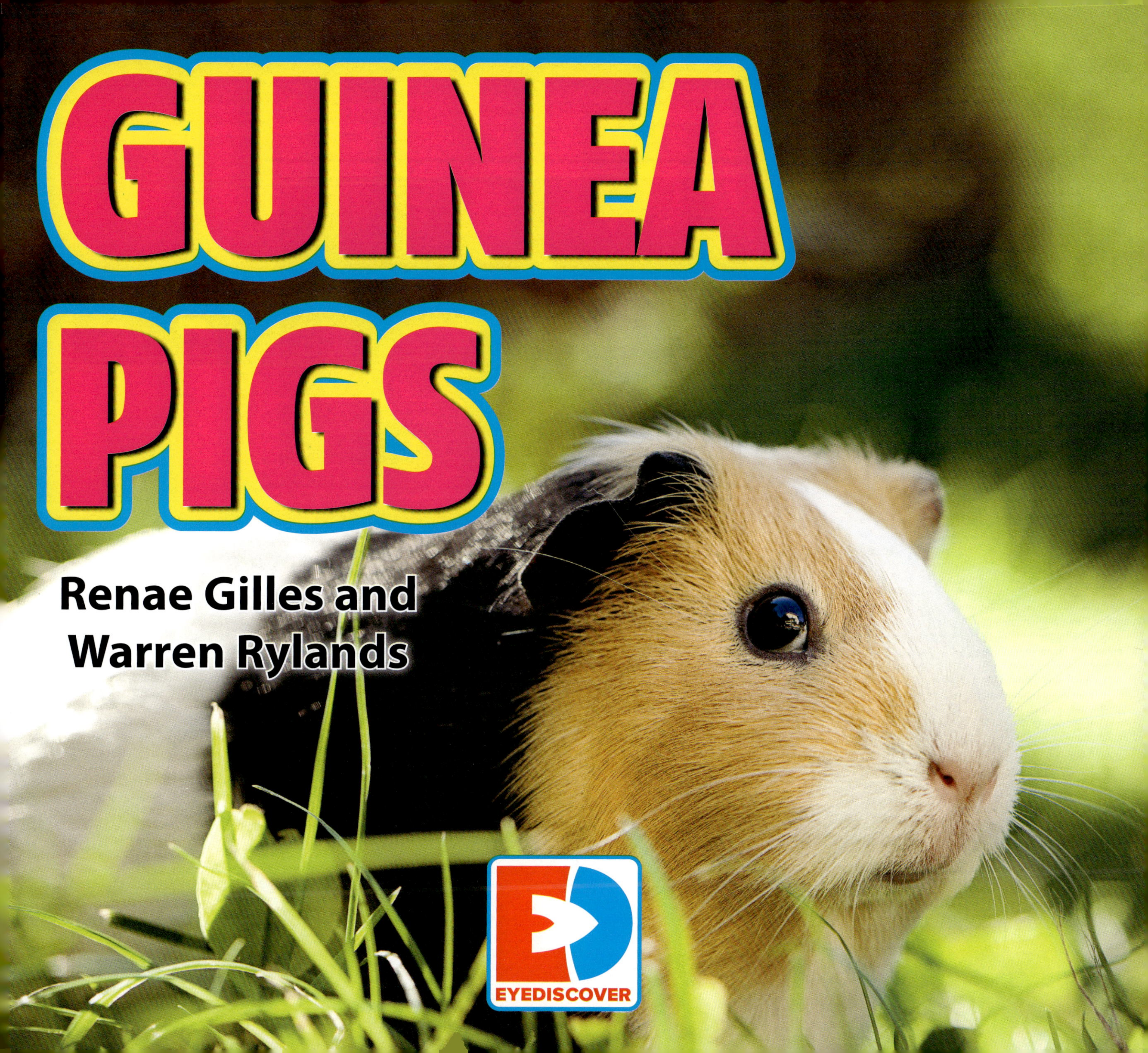
GUINEA
PIGS
Renae Gilles and
Warren Rylands
EYEDISCOVER

Go to **www.eyediscover.com** and enter this book's unique code.

BOOK CODE

AVX89768

EYEDISCOVER brings you optic readalongs that support active learning.

Published by AV² by Weigl
350 5th Avenue, 59th Floor New York, NY 10118
Website: www.eyediscover.com

Library of Congress Control Number: 2018951109

ISBN 978-1-4896-8015-0 (hardcover)

Printed in the United States of America
in Brainerd, Minnesota
1 2 3 4 5 6 7 8 9 0 22 21 20 19 18

082018
120917

Project Coordinator: John Willis
Designer: Mandy Christiansen

Weigl acknowledges Alamy and Shutterstock as the primary image suppliers for this title.

EYEDISCOVER provides enriched content, optimized for tablet use, that supplements and complements this book. EYEDISCOVER books strive to create inspired learning and engage young minds in a total learning experience.

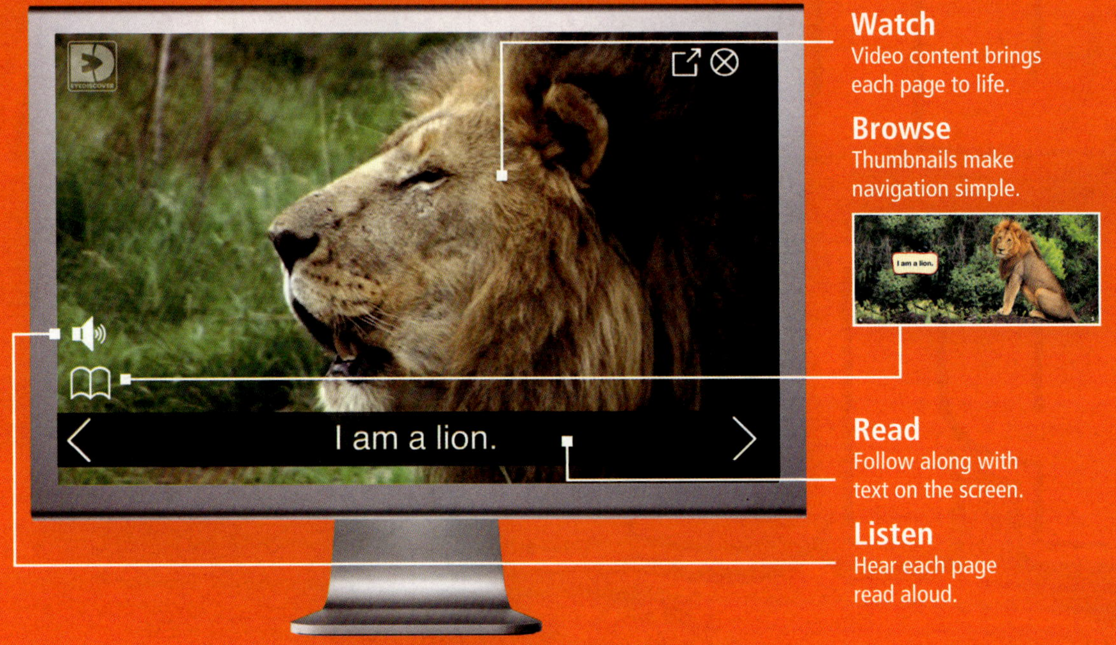

Watch
Video content brings each page to life.

Browse
Thumbnails make navigation simple.

Read
Follow along with text on the screen.

Listen
Hear each page read aloud.

Your EYEDISCOVER Optic Readalongs come alive with...

Audio
Listen to the entire book read aloud.

Video
High resolution videos turn each spread into an optic readalong.

OPTIMIZED FOR

- TABLETS
- WHITEBOARDS
- COMPUTERS
- AND MUCH MORE!

GUINEA PIGS

In this book, you will learn about

- **how they look**
- **where they live**
- **what they do**

and much more!

Guinea pigs are rodents. They are related to squirrels and hamsters.

Guinea pigs first came from South America.

Guinea pigs make many different sounds. They purr, chirp, whistle, and squeal.

Happy guinea pigs hop up and down. This is called popcorning.

Guinea pigs love to be held. They are very popular pets.

Guinea pigs like company. It is best to keep more than one.

Guinea pigs eat fruit, vegetables, and pellets made from hay.

A guinea pig's teeth never stop growing. It needs to chew things to wear them down.

Guinea pigs love to be part of a family. They make great pets.

GUINEA PIGS BY THE NUMBERS

Guinea pigs can have **13 babies** at one time.

Baby guinea pigs can **run** when they are a **few hours old.**

People have kept guinea pigs for more than **3,000** years.

Pet guinea pigs live about **seven** years.

Most guinea pigs have **four** toes on their front feet and **three** toes on their back feet.

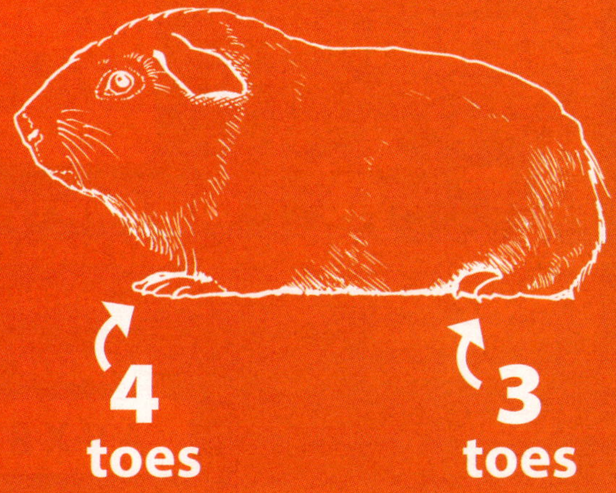

A guinea pig has **five** different types of **hair**.

KEY WORDS

Research has shown that as much as 65 percent of all written material published in English is made up of 300 words. These 300 words cannot be taught using pictures or learned by sounding them out. They must be recognized by sight. This book contains 32 common sight words to help young readers improve their reading fluency and comprehension. This book also teaches young readers several important content words, such as proper nouns. These words are paired with pictures to aid in learning and improve understanding.

Page	Sight Words First Appearance
5	and, are, they, to
6	came, first, from
9	different, make, many
10	down, is, this, up
13	be, very
14	it, keep, like, more, one, than
17	eat, made
18	a, never, stop, them
21	family, great, of, part

Page	Content Words First Appearance
5	guinea pigs, hamsters, rodents, squirrels
6	South America
9	chirp, purr, sounds, squeal, whistle
10	popcorning
13	popular
14	company
17	hay, fruit, pellet, vegetables
18	teeth

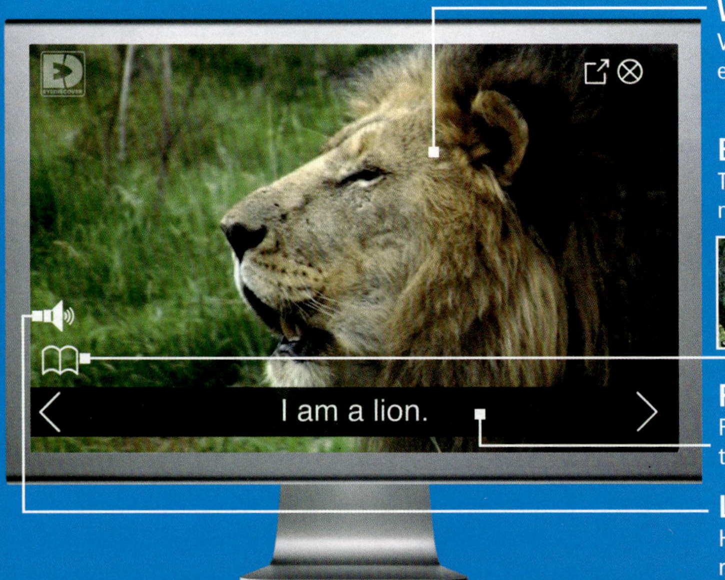

Watch
Video content brings each page to life.

Browse
Thumbnails make navigation simple.

Read
Follow along with text on the screen.

Listen
Hear each page read aloud.

Go to www.eyediscover.com and enter this book's unique code.

BOOK CODE

AVX89768